CHILDREN'S AUTHORS

JEFF KINNEY

Megan M. Gunderson
ABDO Publishing Company

visit us at
www.abdopublishing.com

Published by ABDO Publishing Company, 8000 West 78th Street, Edina, Minnesota 55439.
Copyright © 2012 by Abdo Consulting Group, Inc. International copyrights reserved in all
countries. No part of this book may be reproduced in any form without written permission from the
publisher. The Checkerboard Library™ is a trademark and logo of ABDO Publishing Company.

Printed in the United States of America, North Mankato, Minnesota.
062011
092011
♻ PRINTED ON RECYCLED PAPER
Cover Photo: Getty Images; Interior Photos: AP Images pp. 19, 20; Getty Images pp. 13, 15

Photographs © Wimpy Kid, Inc.
All Rights Reserved.
pp. 5, 6, 7, 8, 11

Diary Of a Wimpy Kid, 2007, p. 16
Diary Of a Wimpy Kid: Rodrick Rules, 2008, p. 9
Diary Of a Wimpy Kid: The Last Straw, 2009, p. 4
Diary Of a Wimpy Kid: Dog Days, 2009, p. 17
Diary Of a Wimpy Kid: Cabin Fever, 2011, p. 21
© Wimpy Kid, Inc.
Diary of a Wimpy Kid and Greg Heffley cover images are trademarks of Wimpy Kid, Inc.
From Diary of a Wimpy Kid Published by Amulet Books, an imprint of Abrams.
All Rights Reserved.

Editors: Tamara L. Britton, BreAnn Rumsch; Art Direction: Neil Klinepier

Library of Congress Cataloging-in-Publication Data

Gunderson, Megan M., 1981-
 Jeff Kinney / Megan M. Gunderson.
   p. cm. -- (Children's authors)
 Includes index.
 ISBN 978-1-61783-048-8
 1. Kinney, Jeff--Juvenile literature. 2. Authors, American--21st century--Biography--Juvenile
literature. 3. Children's stories--Authorship--Juvenile literature. I. Title.
 PS3611.I634Z64 2012
 813'.6--dc22
 [B]
                                      2011011447

CONTENTS

Wimpy Kid Success

Ask adults if they would want to return to middle school, and chances are they'll say absolutely not. For most people, that age is very tough. After all, some kids in school are twice as big as others! That's why author Jeff Kinney decided middle school was the perfect setting for his hilarious books.

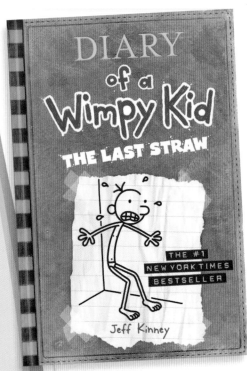

Kinney is the author of the popular Diary of a Wimpy Kid series. Each book in the series is packed with Kinney's jokes and cartoon drawings. The series has caught the attention of readers of all ages. That includes many who were not interested in reading before.

Greg Heffley is the main character in Kinney's books. Greg is not meant to be a great **role model**. Instead, he makes readers laugh. Greg doesn't always make the right decisions. But, readers relate to his "wimpy" moments and love laughing at his misadventures.

Kinney's best-selling books have been published in 30 languages. Millions of copies have been sold around the world!

MARYLAND BOY

Jeff Kinney was born on February 19, 1971, on Andrews Air Force Base in Maryland. He grew up in nearby Fort Washington, Maryland. This is just south of Washington, D.C.

Jeff's father, Brian, worked for the U.S. Navy and later at the Pentagon. He was a military **analyst**. Jeff's mother, Patricia, earned a **PhD** in early childhood development. She worked as a college teacher.

Jeff grew up with an older brother named Scott and an older sister named Annmarie. He also had a younger brother named Patrick.

Jeff knew he wanted to be a cartoonist when he grew up.

Brian, Patricia, Jeff, Annmarie, Patrick, and Scott Kinney (left to right)

As early as age three, Jeff showed an interest in drawing. His first real drawing was of a turtle. By first grade, he was drawing cartoons. He especially admired cartoonist Bill Watterson, who created *Calvin and Hobbes*.

MIDDLE SCHOOL MEMORIES

In fifth grade, Jeff's teacher Mrs. Norton encouraged his sense of humor. She would let students make jokes. But then she would challenge them to be even funnier. Mrs. Norton also recognized and supported Jeff's talent as an illustrator.

For seventh and eighth grade, Jeff attended Eugene Burroughs in Accokeek, Maryland. Jeff was a little awkward in middle school. Like everyone else, he tried hard to fit in.

Jeff **(left)** *at age 11 with his brother Patrick*

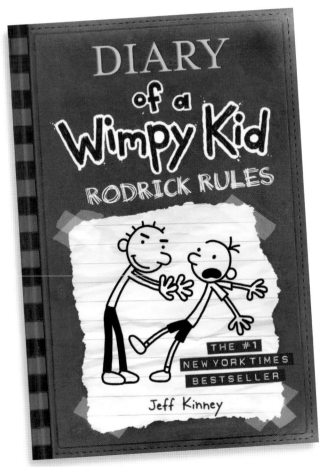

Jeff wrote his brother's summer vacation trick into Diary of a Wimpy Kid. *The toilet paper incident became part of* Diary of a Wimpy Kid: Rodrick Rules.

Many of Jeff's middle school experiences have become part of the Wimpy Kid stories. Just like Greg Heffley, Jeff hid in the bathroom to avoid swim practice. To try to keep warm, he wrapped himself like a mummy in toilet paper!

Another story that ended up in his books happened one summer. Jeff's older brother woke him up in the middle of the night. Scott told him he'd slept through summer vacation. He said Jeff had woken up just in time for school. So Jeff got dressed, went downstairs, and even made breakfast. Then he realized it was two o'clock in the morning and his brother was just kidding!

AVID READER

Jeff grew up surrounded by books. At home, he was never far from good things to read. As a child, Jeff's favorite book was *Tales of a Fourth Grade Nothing* by Judy Blume. He also enjoyed Blume's *Freckle Juice*. He liked how real and funny the characters were.

When he got older, Jeff liked fantasy stories, too. He read *The Lion, the Witch and the Wardrobe* by C.S. Lewis. He also enjoyed *The Hobbit* by J.R.R. Tolkien. Jeff loved stories that took him away to new places. And of course, Jeff also loved funny stories. He read comics like *Calvin and Hobbes* and Gary Larson's *The Far Side*.

After middle school, Jeff attended Bishop McNamara High School in Forestville, Maryland. At the time, it was an all-boys academy. Jeff then won an Air Force **ROTC scholarship** to attend Villanova University in Pennsylvania. There, Jeff would put his cartooning talent to work.

Reading and drawing weren't Jeff's only hobbies. He also participated in Boy Scouts.

COLLEGE COMICS

Kinney only stayed at Villanova for one year. Yet this was an important year for him. Kinney got his comic strip *Igdoof* published in the school's newspaper.

Next, Kinney transferred to the University of Maryland in College Park. The school's newspaper, the *Diamondback*, rejected *Igdoof* at first. But the comic was published during Kinney's last two years there. Soon, it became so popular it was printed in other East Coast college newspapers!

Kinney graduated from the University of Maryland in 1993. Originally, he had studied computer science. But he changed his focus to give himself more time to work on *Igdoof*. Kinney earned a degree in criminal justice. He planned to one day work as a federal law enforcement agent.

Still, *Igdoof* gave Kinney hope that he could become a professional cartoonist. The *Washington Post* even published an article about him. However, he faced one rejection after another. No one was interested in **syndicating** the strip.

So in 1995, Kinney moved to Boston, Massachusetts. He found jobs that put his computer skills to use. Kinney worked as a layout artist for the *Newburyport Daily News* for about three years. Then he worked at a medical **software** company. In 2000, he found a job as a computer-game designer at Family Education Network.

Igdoof introduced Kinney to readers along the East Coast. But the Wimpy Kid books have become popular with readers around the world!

INTRODUCING GREG HEFFLEY

Eventually, Kinney settled in Plainville, Massachusetts. He and his wife, Julie, later had two sons. They are named Will and Grant.

By this time, Kinney was keeping a journal. He included little drawings along with his written words. Kinney realized the combination of cartoons and text could be very fun for people to read. He also decided to start writing about middle school instead of just his daily life. Eventually, this writing would turn into his stories about Greg Heffley.

Kinney decided to make himself fill a 77-page journal with jokes and drawings. That way, he would have enough material to publish just the funniest jokes. This took four years! In spring 2002, Kinney finished filling the journal. Over the next two years, he cut up copies of the pages and pasted them onto poster board to create his story.

Then in 2004, Kinney's boss at Family Education Network needed help with the company's FunBrain.com Web site. He wanted to keep kids interested in it over the summer.

Kinney suggested posting his story on the site. Even using just 20 percent of his material, Kinney had enough to post 1,800 pages of Greg's story on FunBrain.com. Little did he know just how popular it would become!

Kinney and his wife, Julie

BEST-SELLING DIARY

Kinney's *Diary of a Wimpy Kid* cartoon story was very successful at FunBrain.com. Within a year, more than 70,000 people were reading it each day!

Then in 2006, Kinney attended **New York Comic Con**. There, he approached editor Charles Kochman about publishing a book. Kochman immediately loved Kinney's work.

Kinney's first book, *Diary of a Wimpy Kid*, was published in 2007. Critics loved it. And by 2008, the book had sold 1 million copies!

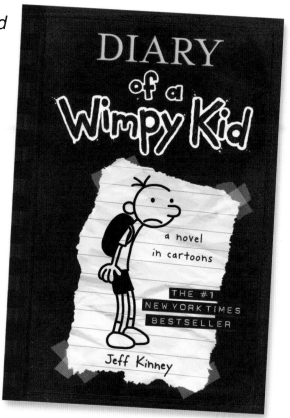

*In German, there's no word for "wimpy." So, the title of Kinney's first book translates as **Greg's Journal: I'm Surrounded by Idiots!***

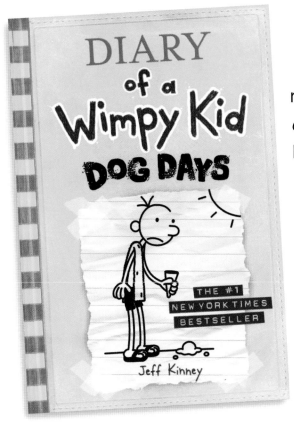

Kinney originally wrote his Greg Heffley stories for adults. But, his publisher suggested putting the books out for kids.

That same year, Kinney released his second book. *Diary of a Wimpy Kid: Rodrick Rules* became a *New York Times* best seller. Also in 2008, Kinney published *The Wimpy Kid Do-It-Yourself Book.* This companion book includes Kinney's drawings along with plenty of space for readers to write their own journal entries.

Kinney's success didn't stop there. The third and fourth books in his Wimpy Kid series were published in 2009. In *Diary of a Wimpy Kid: The Last Straw* readers see Greg trying to prove his father shouldn't send him off to military school. *Diary of a Wimpy Kid: Dog Days* was a fun change for Kinney. Instead of focusing on Greg's school year, the book is about his summer vacation.

From Books to the Big Screen

On March 19, 2010, *Diary of a Wimpy Kid* came to the big screen. It is a live-action movie, but parts of it are **animated**. Kinney was an important part of the filmmaking process. He provided drawings and even created new characters for the animators. He also got to write jokes and make changes to the movie as it was being filmed.

The movie follows the first book fairly closely. However, Kinney learned that some things have to change to make a book into a movie. He loved seeing his book in a new way. Kinney looked forward to working on the second movie, *Diary of a Wimpy Kid: Rodrick Rules*, which would come out just one year later.

To accompany the first movie, Kinney wrote *The Wimpy Kid Movie Diary: How Greg Heffley Went Hollywood*. The book

**Diary of a Wimpy Kid: Rodrick Rules *stars Robert Capron as Rowley,
Zachary Gordon as Greg Heffley, and Devon Bostick as Rodrick* (left to right).**

features Kinney's drawings as well as photographs of the filming process. It shows step-by-step how the book became a movie.

The fifth book in Kinney's series was released November 9, 2010. That first day, *Diary of a Wimpy Kid: The Ugly Truth* sold more than 375,000 copies! The book focuses on Greg's struggles with growing up. But Kinney didn't think his cartoon creation was ready to finish middle school just yet. He wanted to keep telling Greg's story.

More Than an Author

The 2010 Macy's Thanksgiving Day Parade featured a Wimpy Kid balloon.

Today, Kinney still works at Family Education Network. *Diary of a Wimpy Kid* remains a popular part of FunBrain.com.

Kinney also founded and designs content for the Web site Poptropica.com. It features different islands for kids to explore. They can create characters and follow stories in this virtual world.

Even with all those jobs, Kinney remains focused on his family. He spends time with them every day. Then he writes from ten o'clock at night until two o'clock in the morning!

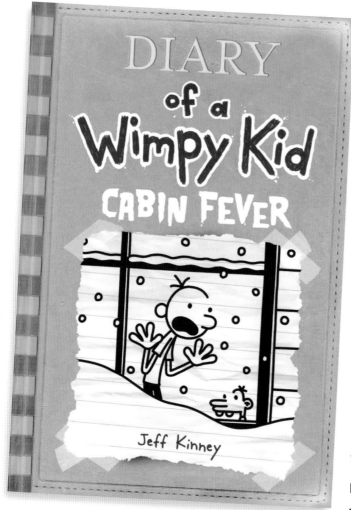

Diary of Wimpy Kid: Cabin Fever came out in 2011. Six million copies were printed for its November release!

Kinney finds both writing and illustrating challenging. Sometimes it takes him four hours to write a single joke. He writes about 600 jokes for each book and only uses half of them. He also creates about 1,000 illustrations for each book!

Because he is so busy, Kinney doesn't get to do many school visits. However, he loves talking to fans. Kinney will keep writing about Greg until he runs out of funny jokes to tell. Readers everywhere hope that doesn't happen anytime soon!

Glossary

analyst - a person who determines the meaning of something by breaking down its parts.

animated - made using a process that involves a projected series of drawings. They appear to move due to slight changes in each drawing. An animator is a person who creates work using this process.

New York Comic Con - a conference in New York City that features comics, graphic novels, video games, movies, television, and author signings.

PhD - doctor of philosophy. Usually, this is the highest degree a student can earn.

role model - a person whose behavior serves as a standard for others to follow.

ROTC - Reserve Officers' Training Corps. ROTC programs train college students for U.S. military service.

scholarship - money or aid given to help a student continue his or her studies.

software - the written programs used to operate a computer.

syndicate (SIHN-duh-kayt) - to sell something for publication in many newspapers or magazines at the same time.

WEB SITES

To learn more about Jeff Kinney, visit ABDO Publishing Company online. Web sites about Jeff Kinney are featured on our Book Links page. These links are routinely monitored and updated to provide the most current information available.
www.abdopublishing.com

INDEX